MY FIRST BOOK
NICARAGUA

ALL ABOUT NICARAGUA FOR KIDS

GLOBED
CHILDREN BOOKS

Interior and cover Design: Daniel Day

Editor: Margaret Bam

For My Sons, Daniel, David and Jude

Granada City, Nicaragua

Nicaragua

Nicaragua is a **country**.

A country is land that is controlled by a **single government**. Countries are also called **nations, states, or nation-states**.

Countries can be **different sizes**. Some countries are big and others are small.

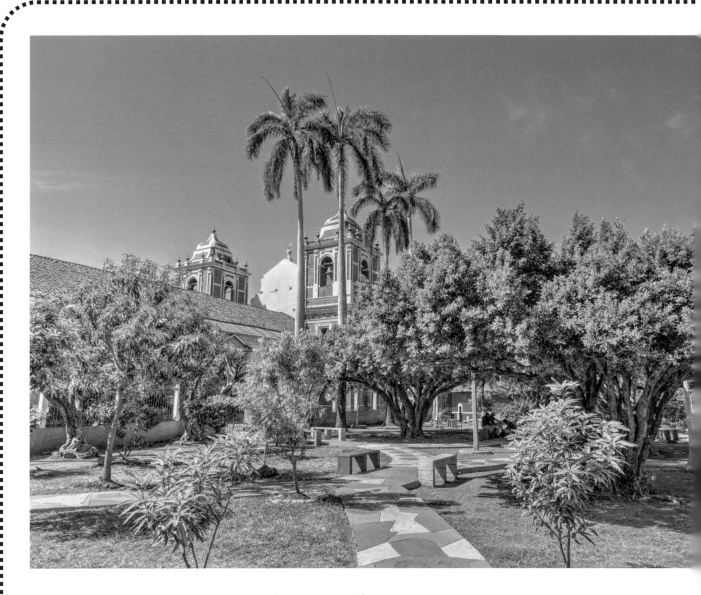

Leon, Nicaragua

Where Is Nicaragua?

Nicaragua is located in the continent of **America**.

A continent is **a massive area of land that is separated from others by water or other natural features**.

Nicaragua is situated in the **central part of America**.

Managua, Nicaragua

Capital

The capital of Nicaragua is **Managua.**

Managua is situated in the western part of the country.

Managua is the largest city in Nicaragua.

Somoto Canyon, Nicaragua

Departments

Nicaragua is divided into 15 departments

The departments of Nicaragua are:

Boaco, Carazo, Chinandega, Chontales, Estelí, Granada, Jinotega, León, Madriz, Managua, Masaya, Matagalpa, Nueva Segovia, Rivas, and Río San Juan.

Population

Nicaragua has population of around **6.3 million people.**

The most populous city in Nicaragua is Managua, which is also the capital city and home to approximately 1.4 million people. The majority of the population (about 60%) lives in urban areas, while the remaining 40% live in rural areas.

Bus in Nicaragua

Size

Nicaragua is **130,375 square kilometres** making it the 96th largest country in the world and the largest country in Central America.

Nicaragua is bordered by Honduras to the north, the Caribbean to the east, Costa Rica to the south, and the Pacific Ocean to the west.

Languages

The official language of Nicaragua is Spanish, which is spoken by the majority of the population. There are also regional languages spoken throughout the country, including English, Miskito, Rama, Sumo, Miskito Coast Creole, Garifuna and Rama Cay Creole.

Here are a few Spanish phrases

- **¿Cómo estás?- How are you?**
- **Mucho gusto - Nice to meet you**
- **¿Qué tal? – How are you?**
- **¿Qué pasa? – What's up?**

Lake Nicaragua

Attractions

There are lots of interesting places to see in Nicaragua.

Some beautiful places to visit in Nicaragua are

- **Apoyo Lagoon Natural Reserve**
- **Islets of Granada**
- **Teatro Nacional Rubén Darío**
- **Cristo de La Misericordia**
- **Lake Nicaragua**

History of Nicaragua

Nicaragua has a long and complex history that dates back thousands of years. Nicaragua was originally inhabited by various indigenous groups, including the Nahuatl, Chibcha, and Lenca people.

Nicaragua was colonized by the Spanish in the 16th century and after more than 300 years of Spanish rule, Nicaragua gained its independence in 1821.

In the late 19th and early 20th centuries, Nicaragua experienced a series of political upheavals and civil wars, including the U.S. military intervention in the country.

El Gueguense, Nicaraguan folklore mask

Customs

Nicaragua has many fascinating customs and traditions.

- **Semana Santa is a significant religious event in Nicaragua. During this time, many Nicaraguans participate in processions.**
- **An important tradition in Nicaragua is the celebration of patron saints, which takes place in cities and towns throughout the country.**
- **Nicaragua has a rich and diverse folklore; one example is El Güegüense which tells the story of a mestizo man who outwits Spanish colonial authorities.**

Music

Music and dance play a significant role in Nicaraguan culture, with a variety of traditional styles including marimba music, son nica, and the national dance, El Güegüense.

Some notable Nicaraguan musicians include
- **Carlos Mejía Godoy - A Nicaraguan musician, composer and singer-songwriter.**
- **Luis Enrique Mejía López - A Nicaraguan-American singer-songwriter and composer.**
- **Alfonso Noel Lovo - A Nicaraguan composer and guitarist.**

Nicaragua food of rice, beans, salad and plantains

Food of Nicaragua

Nicaraguan cuisine is known for its unique blend of indigenous, Spanish, and Creole influences, resulting in a diverse range of flavours and dishes. The country's cuisine is characterized by the use of fresh, locally-sourced ingredients

Some popular dishes in Nicaragua include
- **Gallo pinto - A traditional breakfast dish made with rice and beans cooked together**
- **Sopa de Mondongo - A hearty soup made with tripe, vegetables, and spices**
- **Indio Viejo - A stew made with shredded beef, cornmeal, tomatoes, onions, and peppers.**

Statue of Ruben Dario, Managua, Nicaragua

Weather

Nicaragua has a **tropical climate**, with average temperatures ranging from 25 to 30 degrees Celsius throughout the year. The country experiences two seasons: a dry season from November to April, and a rainy season from May to October.

Nicaragua is vulnerable to natural disasters such as hurricanes and earthquakes.

Jaguar

Animals

There are many wonderful animals in Nicaragua.

Here are some animals that live in Nicaragua

- Common iguana
- Jaguar
- Reptiles
- Jaguarundi
- Ocelot
- Armadillo

Little Corn Island

Beaches

There are many beautiful beaches in Nicaragua which is one of the reasons why so many people visit this beautiful country every year.

Here are some of Nicaragua's beaches

- **Yemaya, Little Corn Island**
- **Playa Maderas**
- **Redonda Bay**
- **Playa El Coco**
- **Las Peñitas**
- **Pearl Cays**

Nicaragua football fan

Sports

Soccer is the most popular sport in Nicasragua. The sport is deeply ingrained in the culture and has a strong following among all ages.

Here are some of famous sportspeople from Nicaragua

- Alexis Argüello - Boxing
- Denis Espinoza - Football
- Juan Barrera - Football
- David Solórzano - Football

Augusto Sandino

Famous

Nicaragua has been home to many notable figures in various fields.

Here are a few examples

- **Augusto Sandino - Revolutionary**
- **Ruben Dario - Nicaraguan poet**
- **German Pomares - Revolutionary**
- **Carlos Fonseca - Teacher, librarian and revolutionary**

San Juan Del Sur Resort, Nicaragua

Something Extra...

As a little something extra, we are going to share some lesser known facts about Nicaragua.

- Nicaragua is home to the second-largest rainforest in the Americas, after the Amazon, known as the Bosawás Biosphere Reserve.
- The national flower of Nicaragua is the sacuanjoche, a fragrant yellow flower also known as the plumeria.
- Nicaragua is one of the few places in the world where you can go volcano boarding, which involves sliding down the side of a volcano on a wooden board.

Nicaraguan child

Words From the Author

We hope that you enjoyed learning about the wonderful country of Nicaragua.

Nicaragua is a country rich in culture and beauty, with lots of wonderful places to visit and people to meet.

We hope you continue to learn more about this wonderful nation. If you enjoyed this book, consider leaving a review!

With Love

For My Sons, Daniel Zachary and Jack

Printed in Great Britain
by Amazon

44306427R00025